North American
Animals

WOLVES

by Michael Dahl

Consulting Editor: Gail Saunders-Smith, PhD

CAPSTONE PRESS
a capstone imprint

Pebble Plus is published by Capstone Press,
1710 Roe Crest Drive, North Mankato, Minnesota 56003.
www.capstonepub.com

Books published by Capstone Press are manufactured with paper
containing at least 10 percent post-consumer waste.

Library of Congress Cataloging-in-Publication Data
Dahl, Michael.
  Wolves / by Michael Dahl.
      p. cm.—(Pebble plus. North American animals)
  Includes bibliographical references and index.
  Summary: "Simple text and full-color photographs provide a brief introduction to wolves"—Provided by publisher.
  ISBN 978-1-4296-7701-1 (library binding)
  ISBN 978-1-4296-7925-1 (paperback)
  1. Wolves—North America—Juvenile literature. I. Title. II. Series.
  QL737.C22D344 2012
  599.773097—dc23   2011025653

Editorial Credits
Erika L. Shores, editor; Heidi Thompson, designer; Svetlana Zhurkin, media researcher;
    Kathy McColley, production specialist

Photo Credits
Alamy: First Light, 18–19; Dreamstime: Denis Pepin, 9, Eric Inghels, cover, Jean-Edouard Rozey, 6–7; National
Geographic Stock: Jim and Jamie Dutcher, 13; Photolibrary: Thomas Kitchin and Victoria Hurst, 15; Shutterstock:
Al Parker Photography, 10–11, Holly Kuchera, 1, Lori Labrecque, 17, Ronnie Howard, 21, S.R. Maglione, 5

Note to Parents and Teachers

The North American Animals series supports national science standards related to life science.
This book describes and illustrates wolves. The images support early readers in understanding
the text. The repetition of words and phrases helps early readers learn new words. This book
also introduces early readers to subject-specific vocabulary words, which are defined in the
Glossary section. Early readers may need assistance to read some words and to use the Table of
Contents, Glossary, Read More, Internet Sites, and Index sections of the book.

Printed in the United States of America in North Mankato, Minnesota.
112012   006 5

Table of Contents

Living in North America

Wolves roam forests, deserts, and mountains. In North America, most wolves are gray wolves. They live in Canada and the northern United States.

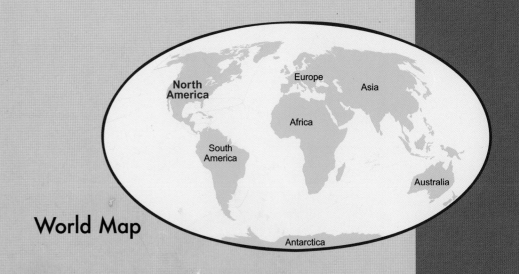

World Map

The red wolf is the other kind
of North American wolf.
It lives only in North Carolina.
Fewer than 100 red wolves live
in the wild.

North America Map

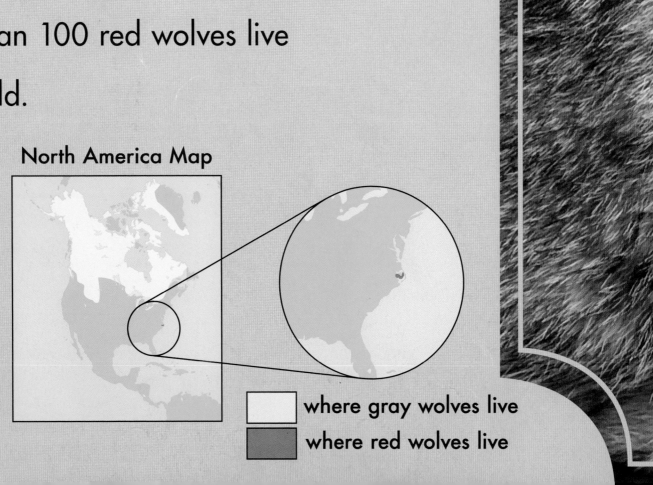

where gray wolves live
where red wolves live

Up Close!

A wolf's coat blends with its
surroundings. Wolves living in
forests have a mix of white,
black, brown, and gray fur.
In the Arctic, wolves are white.

Wolves are dangerous
predators. They have
strong legs, powerful jaws,
and sharp teeth.

Eating

Wolves hunt together in packs.

They sniff out prey

from miles away.

Wolves eat mice, rabbits,

deer, elk, and moose.

The pack chases and surrounds
prey before attacking. The pack
shares what they kill.
Their sharp teeth chew up
meat and bones.

Growing Up

The male and female pack
leaders mate in early spring.
A litter of four to six pups
is born about 60 days later.

At first, pups stay safe in a den. Older wolves in the pack bring them food. Young wolves begin to travel with the pack after one year.

Staying Safe

People are wolves' greatest enemy.
Farmers kill wolves that come
near livestock. Other people build
on land where wolves live.
Laws protect wolves in some areas.

Glossary

Arctic—the area near the North Pole; the Arctic is cold and covered with ice

den—a place where a wild animal may live; a female wolf gives birth to pups and keeps them safe in dens

livestock—animals raised to sell

mate—to join together to produce young

pack—a small group of animals that lives and hunts together; most wolves live in packs while others live alone

predator—an animal that hunts other animals for food

prey—an animal hunted by another animal for food

Read More

Barnes, Julia. *The Secret Lives of Wolves*. The Secret Lives of Animals. Milwaukee: Gareth Stevens Pub., 2007.

Brandenburg, Jim, and Judy Brandenburg. *Face to Face with Wolves*. Face to Face with Animals. Washington, D.C.: National Geographic, 2008.

Hudak, Heather C., ed. *Wolves*. Backyard Animals. New York: Weigl Publishers Inc., 2009.

Internet Sites

FactHound offers a safe, fun way to find Internet sites related to this book. All of the sites on FactHound have been researched by our staff.

Here's all you do:

Visit *www.facthound.com*

Type in this code: 9781429677011

Check out projects, games and lots more at
www.capstonekids.com

Super-cool stuff!

Index

Word Count: 201
Grade: 1
Early-Intervention Level: 20